MANCHESTER 100 YEARS AGO

by
CLIFF HAYES

Introducing the places and people of
Manchester in the 1890's

PRINTWISE PUBLICATIONS LIMITED
1993

Copyright 1993
PRINTWISE PUBLICATIONS LIMITED
47 Bradshaw Road, Tottington, Bury,
Lancs, BL8 3PW.

Warehouse & Orders
Unit 9c, Bradley Fold Trading Estate,
Radcliffe Moor Road,
BOLTON BL2 6RT.
Tel: 0204 370 753
Fax: 0204 370 751

Text written and illustrations selected by

liff Hayes

ISBN No. 1 872226 66 3

This book is based on a series of magazines called
MANCHESTER FACES & PLACES (1889–1895)   05776727

Printed and Bound by:
Manchester Free Press, Longford Trading Estate,
Thomas Street, Stretford, Manchester M32 0JT.
Tel: 061 864 4540   Fax: 061 866 9866

ABOUT THE AUTHOR

Born in 1945 and brought up in The Ball O'Ditton, Widnes, when it was proper and part of Lancashire. Educated at Chestnut Lodge Infants, Simms Cross Junior and then Wade Deacon Grammar School in Widnes he then spent 4 years going to nightschool at The College of Art in Liverpool to study Printing, design and english.

From the age. of 13, he has been involved in printing, working part-time at a small local printers, then getting an apprenticeship at Swale Press (Widnes Weekly News, Runcorn, Liverpool etc.) then started helping and writing for Mersey Beat and also writing a disc and pop column for the Weekly News.

Letchworth; Tinlings, Prescott: Ship's Printer, Canadian Pacific to Canada and Cruising, Shaw Saville on Round the World trips and Japanese/Australian cruising etc; Book production in Blackpool; newspaper works manager in the Isle of Man; lino operator on National Newspapers (The Daily Mirror; The Sporting Chronicle, The Daily Telegraph etc.); computer training and 12 months as print salesman all added to a broad view of every aspect of life in general.

Now settled in Manchester for the last 20 years, happily married with a teenage daughter, Cliff took up publishing 5 years ago and then progressed to writing books. This is his seventh book though he has co-written eight more.

Grateful Thanks to Tony Gibb for selling me the set of Faces .and Places, Jimmy McGill for the additional material and Sylvia my wife for typing and sometimes editing the manuscript.

ABOUT THE MAGAZINE

All the pictures used in this book come from a magazine called 'Manchester Faces & Places' published at 6d a month by a company called J.G. Hammon & Company whose offices were at 44 Corporation Street.

Recent changes and advancements in printing made pictures (block making) cheaper and better and it was possible to produce reasonably cheaply a clear likeness of the photographs of the day.

It would be nice to report that it was a local Company but they seemed to have been a Birmingham Company who had success with 'Birmingham Faces' and had decided to expand to London and Manchester. The first edition was October 1889 and the magazine ran for about 10 years finishing late 1900 but carrying advertisements and featuring more of Wales and the Lancashire coast than the Cities.

The articles in it were 'placed' with many different authors and the pen-sketches of prominent Mancunians were often written by the subject themselves, or at least dictated by them. While the magazine is a wonderful record of Manchester in the 1890's be very careful when using it as research material, there are quite a few articles which must have been written by people the publishers did not wish to offend as they have been included but are very inaccurate. Yet there are others which shed new light on the city's past. Always try and cross-check your facts with another source. I have tried to and I hope I have got my facts right or most of them anyway. I have tried to straighten out one or two little mysteries and mistakes that seem to be creeping in. I heard a guide telling that the Albert Memorial was given by Abel Heywood, yet I knew that it was not, and it took research from three different angles to get the true story (inside). I hope you think the research has been worth while.

INTRODUCTION

The title "Manchester 100 Years Ago" has been used before. Three times at least and I have no doubt that it will be used again. So why this book, and why now?

Manchester has taken on an air of change. The trams are back, the planning of the Olympic Games, and the city has recognised some of the planning mistakes of the 1960's and 70's, and is trying to put them right. There is definitely an air of 'community' coming back to this great city. The year 2000 is now firmly on the horizon and approaching with increasing certainty. Before we reach that date I would like you to join me in the Manchester that was approaching 1900 (the 20th century). Looking at the city then I was amazed how alike the two eras are. Manchester was a very young city, and was trying to be the best at all it did and built. Trams were just about to come onto the streets, telephones were being used more and more, which meant wholesale lay-offs amongst the 'runners' in the Town Hall and in the business community, as messages could now be telephoned. The Ship Canal was almost ready and the promise of employment for thousands brought relief to Salford and Manchester where 10,000 jobs were created when it finally did open.

Victoria was still on the throne, but unlike our present Queen she did not get out much. She refused to come to Manchester, and there were mutterings for her abdication. One of the reasons why feelings on the subject of her abdication were not expressed more forcefully was because Edward, who had waited for most of his adult life to ascend the throne was not the man that most of ruling Britain wanted. Everybody knew about his play-boy life style, but the many scandals were kept very quiet, and the newspapers of the day stuck together and did the decent thing by not mentioning them. So Queen Victoria stayed on the throne despite all the mutterings, until her death in 1901. So much changes yet so much history repeats itself.

Look at Manchester with its council fighting over lay-offs and cut-backs, worries about rising crime rates, bad housing, immigration, worries about people's health with the increase in mechanisation and new technology, and the ever widening gap between the Have and Have-nots, yes, Manchester 1894!

There is always a danger of putting too much detail and facts in these books, yet there are people and facts that need to be noted and remembered. And so I have tried to strike a balance, and bring back to life my Manchester heroes and my Manchester curiosities, and I hope you enjoy the journey to . . .

. . . MANCHESTER 100 YEARS AGO

DEDICATION

In 1986 when the newspapers in Manchester were changing to new technology I was helping in the Printing Department of the Museum of Science & Industry. I was helping to save lino-type machines, stones and all the fast disappearing trappings of hot-metal printing.

There were two men working there whom it was my pleasure and honour to get to know. Although both have now sadly passed on, I would like to dedicate this book to them - JACK RICHARDS and BERT DRING.

Jack was a printer of the old school, a gentleman of the press who could make the old machines sing, while Bert (a self taught printer) was a very kind and gentle person whose patience with the young visitors to the Museum was a treat for all.

To: JACK AND BERT

MARKET STREET, MANCHESTER.

Looking up Market Street from Corporation Street, the horse-drawn omnibuses heading across to Cheetham Hill or up the slope into Piccadilly. J. S. Moss & Son's shop on the left corner is just where Burton's Top Shop is today. Market Stead Lane this street used to be called before it was widened a hundred years before.

So much was peoples' sympathy for Queen Victoria's loss of her beloved Albert that when thoughts of a Memorial were first mooted it was felt a special area should be cleared for the tribute. So Albert Square was created, for the sole purpose of showing the Memorial off to its best advantage and giving necessary honour.

There is quite a lot of confusion over this Memorial, to clarify the facts you must think of it in two separate parts. Firstly there is the statue itself, which bears the grand title of "Albert the Good" which was commissioned by Alderman Thomas Goadsby who paid the sculptor Matthew Noble to produce the statue shortly after Prince Albert's death. Unfortunately before the statue was finished Thomas Goadsby had died. His widow went on to marry Abel Heywood, and it was as Mrs Abel Heywood that she presented the statue to the people of Manchester, but it was her first husband Mr Goadsby who had commissioned it and paid for it.

The outside and the Memorial tower itself was paid for by public subscription, but the Chairman of the Committee was Abel Heywood so he sometimes gets the credit. The grand amount of £6,250.00 was raised to pay for this 75ft high tribute which was designed by Thomas Worthington and presented to the people of Manchester on 23rd January 1867.

A fine photograph looking across Albert Square to the Town Hall. This was the second Town Hall, but the first specifically built for that purpose. Designed by Alfred Waterhouse, the foundation stone was laid with great ceremony on Monday 26th October 1868 by the Mayor Robert Neill. Under the stone were placed copies of the latest London and Manchester papers, the coins of the day, and other Council paraphernalia. The topping off was done in December 1875. Seven years to build, and then two years to fit out and furnish, the building cost £480,000. including fixtures and fittings, plus another £300,000. to buy and clear the 8000 square yards on land it stood on.

The side facing the square is the main entrance and is 328ft long though the Princess Street facade is longer at 388ft. At the height of building activity in 1870 there were over 1,000 builders and 700 masons (many imported from Italy who stayed in the town) working on the building. Over 480,000 cubic feet of stone brought from Bradford was used to clad the $16\frac{1}{2}$ million (16,500,000.) bricks.

MR. ALDERMAN HEYWOOD.
Father of the Manchester Corporation.

One of my heroes, this man, I don't think history gives him enough praise or credit.

Born in 1810 in Prestwich. His widowed mother moved into Manchester when he was nine years old, with the object of earning a living. After various jobs he opened a half-penny reading room which was an immediate success, he then went into the book trade and opened a shop on Oldham Street. Reading rooms grew up because although newspapers cost only 2d the 4d tax that was added to that proved too high a cost for most people to buy their own papers. Heywood called it a "tax on knowledge" and backed a political journal called 'The Poor Man's Guardian' upon which he sold minus the 4d tax. It was his opposition to the Governments tax of 4d on every newspaper that lead to his spending four months in the New Bailey Prison. On release he still campaigned for the repeal of the tax and six years later it was reduced to a penny. He believed in easy access to literature for everyone and did much for education.

In 1836 he was elected as one of the Commissioners on the Police Committee who also ran the Gas, the Street Lighting, the Sanitation and much more besides. He led from the front and helped bring in many amenities which were of great benefit to the general public. He was twice Mayor of Manchester and Chairman of the Committee that planned and built the Town Hall off Albert Square and it was a fitting climax when he opened the main door officially with the golden key in 1877. Many people thought and said it was a great pity that Queen Victoria had declined to open the Town Hall as Councillor Heywood would surely have become Sir Abel Heywood.

When the Town Hall was first built it contained apartments for the Mayor who moved in once elected and more or less lived there during his year of office. This was the case when this picture of the Mayor's Parlour was taken in 1892, and Anthony Marshal J.P. was the Mayor. He was the last Mayor of Manchester. The title Lord Mayor was granted in 1893.

CITY COUNCIL CHAMBER, MANCHESTER TOWN HALL.

A clear picture of the City Council Chamber in the Town Hall with its ornate ceilings and fine iron work. Everywhere, in the tile work, the plaster work, even in the intricate iron work, is depicted the cotton flower, which brought so much wealth to Manchester, and the Bee, symbolic of Manchester as a hive of industry. A surprising bonus nowadays is the number of times this building, and especially this room is used for filming. A grade one listed building, well worth your consideration and very rewarding to those with time to stroll around it. Have you ever looked up and seen what is right on top of the Town Hall clock tower? Look for yourself you'll be surprised.

There are 23 bells hung in the Tower, ten of the bells were hung as a ringing peel and are the same as the famous Bow Bells. Each of the bells were each given the initial of a member of the Council or Corporation of that year and also a line from Tennyson's poem 'Ring Out Wild Bells'. The largest one (G) weighs 6ton 9cwts the 4th largest in England and bears the initials AH for Abel Heywood, and the first line of the poem which is "Ring out the false, ring in the true".

There were many problems when the bells first rang out. The tower had to be re-pointed twice due to the strength of the sound of the peel. There is a keyboard (A Carion) that enables tunes to be played on these bells and although it was much used in the 1890's and even after the war were used on special occasions. At the moment it is broken, but maybe this would be a good time to consider repairing the mechanism then the bells could ring out to welcome Manchester's successful Olympic bid.

Ring out the false, ring in the true.
Ring out the grief that saps the mind,
    For those that here we see no more ;—
    Ring out the feud of rich and poor,
Ring in redress to all mankind.

GREAT HOUR BELL.

SMITHYDOOR MARKET, MANCHESTER.

This is a very old part of the City and was at one time its centre. The window of the Wellington Inn, at that time a Fishing Tackle shop, can be made out middle left. The stalls selling flowers & plants are on the spot of the former Shambles where butchers and slaughterers once plied their trade.

To work out where this area was, stand in St. Mary's Gate and face the door of Marks and Spencer (the door that leads down to the food hall) and you are stood where the photographer stood to take this picture. The buildings in the background are in Cateaton Street and Cathedral Street.

PICCADILLY, MANCHESTER.

Once known as Portland Place. In 1890 the main building was the Infirmary and Infirmary pond which was 615ft long. The corner of Oldham Street is on the right. It was *THE* street for ladies' fashions and accessories. Thomas Houldsworth's town house had just been converted into the Queen's Hotel, other hotels around Portland Place were The Royal Hotel, The Albion and the very old but jovial White Bear Hotel.

This photograph taken from the second floor of Lewis's building looking towards Portland Street and Piccadilly Station.

MANCHESTER ASSIZE COURTS.

What a fine and noble building was Manchester's Assize Courts. It stood on the right as you head up Great Ducie Street. The street on the right is Southall Street and in fact the smaller building on that street on the right is the main entrance to Strangeways Jail and is still there, which helps place this magnificent 256ft long building. In 1858 The Hundred of Salford was ordered to erect "lodgings for judges, offices and lock-ups and all other necessary accommodation needed for holding civil and criminal assizes". Alfred Waterhouse who went on to build the Town Hall designed the Courts and later the Jail. An old mansion, Strangeways Hall, and its land were purchased to provide the space for the Courts and Jail. It is a quirk of fate that the name of the Strangweys family and the lovely Strangeways Hall now is given to an infamous prison which has gone into history for the riots there in 1990. The building was hit by incendiary bombs during the second world war and was completely destroyed.

THE FREE TRADE HALL.

To get the real meaning of the name of this building you should try referring to it as the Hall dedicated to FREE TRADE for that is why it was built. Stand opposite this square squat building and you are standing on the site of Peterloo, and the Anti-Corn Law demonstrations of 1819. It was almost called the Guild Hall, in fact the deeds for this building have Guild Hall on them.

The Hall was opened on 10th October 1856 and cost £40,000. At the time of this photograph the Hall could seat 3,165 people and was always filled to capacity by people wishing to hear the great reformers, thinkers and writers in the days before radio and television.

During World War II, Churchill spoke here to rally the workers of Manchester and revisited only months later when it was badly damaged in an air raid.

In 1986 new technology meant mass lay-offs in the printing industry, and when Robert Maxwell bid for the Mirror Group and Thomson House, all the N.G.A. (printers) gathered here to discuss how or if they would fight. I remember as I listened to the reassurances that 'he wouldn't get away with it' thinking of all the other debates that had gone on in the same manner, with the same urgency, in the same great Hall.

ST. ANN'S SQUARE.

The Square in 1891 taken from the tower of St. Ann's Church. This is one of Manchester's most historic spots. I could fill a book with just the history of this area. Once known as Acres Field in the 1600s and was the site of a great three day market and fair held on St.Matthew's day (September 21st) and for two days after. The Square started with the building of the Church in 1709 and the buildings on the left were started around 1735. It was in this Square just where the cabs are that Bonny Prince Charlie reviewed his troops before marching south. It was in this Square also that he declared himself 'King James III'. If you stand outside Waterstone's Bookshop you are standing on the very spot of the first elections for M.P.'s. No ballot votes then, just a full day of speeches and barracking followed by a show of hands for each candidate and that was it, you had two M.P.'s and the first two for Manchester were Philips and Poulett.

St. Ann's Square was the gathering place for the first Whit Walks in 1809 when they came to the Square to a bread and cheese repast. All mileages to and from Manchester were measured from the far side of this Square and as far as I know still are. At the time of this photograph it was *The* shopping Square.

"YE OLD SEVEN STARRS," WITHY GROVE, MANCHESTER.
(Licensed over 500 years.)

The loss of the 'Seven Starrs Inn' from Withy Grove is one of the planning sins of Manchester. Only 20 years after this picture was taken the Inn was dismantled and sold as Ancient building material by auction on 18th July 1911. The most historic ale house in the city just sold off. Admittedly some of its legends and facts were a little dubious and exaggerated, but to lose so much history just to widen a road was a scandal. The landlord when this picture was taken, William Henry Shaw, was happily showing visitors "Ye Traditional Chamber" with beams so low you could touch them, and buxom wenches dispensing hospitality in worthy fashion. 'Ye Vestry' a room with bricked-up arch which the Landlord said was the start of a passage that gave subterranean communication with the Collegiate Church, now Manchester Cathedral, supposed to have been used not only by the workmen who built the church but by the infamous Guy Fawkes to escape across the river to Ordsall Hall. There was also the 'Guy Fawkes Chamber'.

All this folklore was much strengthened by Harrison Ainsworth's novel 'Guy Fawkes' which named the Seven Starrs. The Inn claimed to have first been licenced in 1350, but since the first licence for a public house was 1551 it was probably from then, which still made it 350 years old. When the Inn was demolished the passage were looked for but not found. Note the two 'R's in the Inn's name and on the board.

The name Withy Grove comes from Withingreave Hall which was at the top on the right (just where the tram tracks cross the road) and the Seven Starrs was half-way down on the left where the buses come out of the Bus Station now.

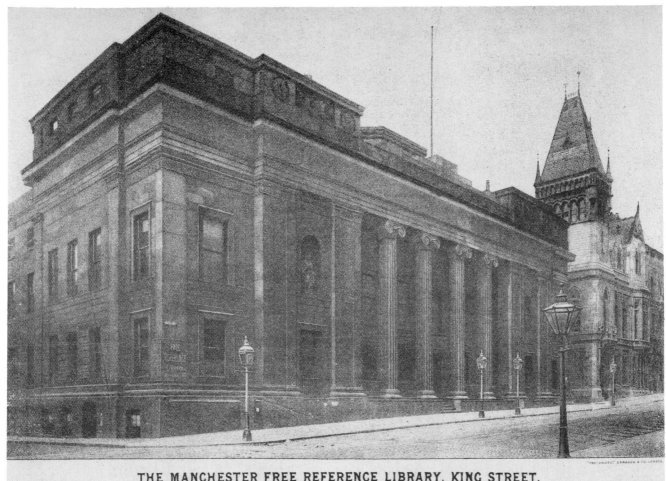

THE MANCHESTER FREE REFERENCE LIBRARY, KING STREET.

Manchester Free Library was on the corner of King Street and Cross Street. The building, started around 1825, had previously been the Town Hall until 1877 when the new Town Hall was opened in Albert Square. The top part of King Street was once known as St. James's Street, named to keep the Pretender's name on the lips of the Jacobites in Manchester, but after the events of 1745 the name was dropped and King Street (the name for the bottom end) extended to the whole Street. Also on this site in the early eighteenth century was Dr. White's house. Dr. White was connected with the Jacobites in 1715 and 1745. It was Dr. White, a famous physician who founded Manchester's first Infirmary. This building was pulled down when it was sold to Lloyds Bank in 1904, and the pillars were removed to Heaton Park where they remain today. Just in passing the towers so prominent next door belonged to the District Bank.

Opened to the public at the same time as Peel Park and Philips Park in 1846.

Queen's Park and its Museum and Art Gallery was gaining much popularity with the residents of Harpurhey, and Sundays and holidays would find plenty of folk parading its level plateaux, dells and cloughs and small wood. It cost £6,500 to build the Museum and lay out the 30 acre Park.

QUEEN'S PARK, HARPURHEY, MANCHESTER.

THE ROYAL INFIRMARY, PICCADILLY, MANCHESTER.

This was the scene in Piccadilly Gardens in 1890. The Royal Infirmary with its high dome and clock faces lords over a well laid out and neat Square. A lake and fountains which had so delighted Queen Victoria 40 years earlier had just been filled in and paved over. The building had been a hospital of sorts since 1755 and was made up of three parts, the Hospital, the Asylum, and a Public Bath House. The patients were moved out on Tuesday 1st September 1908 when a large crowd gathered to watch about 100 patients carried out to ambulances. Only one patient was left behind because he was too ill to move. The main building was demolished, and the outbuildings became a reference library and many and long were the arguments over the future of the square.

Founded by Humphrey Chetham in 1651 this is one view of Manchester that has remained the same, not for a 100 years but for nearer 300 years. Humphrey Chetham left £7,000 in his will to provide a fund to educate 40 poor children from 6-14 years of age. "They must be the children of poor, but honest parents, not deceased at the time of choosing, not lame or blind. The boys chosen to have diet, lodging, apparel and instruction."

He loved books and wished to pass on that joy and left £1,000. to create a Library at the school, and £100. to build a place to keep the books, £200 for the churches in the Manchester district to buy 'good' books and ALL the remainder of his estate to increase the books in the Library. At the time of this photograph the number of boys had increased to about 100 and on every Easter Monday those whom their teachers thought had completed their education bade a formal farewell whilst those thought worthy to join were brought before the Head and any vacant rooms were filled.

CHETHAM COLLEGE, MANCHESTER.

This was the second building to carry the name the Manchester Exchange and upon Queen Victoria's and Prince Albert's dining here in 1851, she graciously allowed it to be called the ROYAL Exchange.

The first Exchange was at the mouth of St. Ann's Square, and had been dismantled a hundred years before in 1793. The present Exchange is this one plus an extension from the 1920's.

MANCHESTER ROYAL EXCHANGE.

The view of the Manchester Royal Exchange from Cross Street showing the Portico Entrance which was its principal front. This fine building also contained the first Telephone Exchange which was situated at the top of the building, the telegraph poles can be seen fixed on the roof. The dome of Barton Arcade can just be seen on the skyline.

MANCHESTER ROYAL EXCHANGE, PRINCIPAL FRONT.

MANCHESTER ROYAL EXCHANGE.

(From a Photograph by Messrs. Frith & Sons, Reigate.)

It was announced in March 1892 that the Royal Exchange had decided to remove the large ornate portico that adorned Cross Street, and extend the front of the building to come into line with the newly emerging Cross Street/Corporation Street. This would provide more rooms for the growing membership and the cost of £14,000 was to be borne by the members. The original architect James Murgatroyd was brought back to do the job. This picture shows the main hall (the largest and most commodious exchange in the world) looking towards the Cross Street entrance. The 120ft high dome looked down on a busy exchange especially on Tuesday and Fridays which were 'Market Days'.

A strong classic building in academic style, it was the home of Henshaw's Blind Asylum, founded through the benevolence of Thomas Henshaw in 1837. It was children who were housed, treated and looked after here and The Henshaw's Workshop still exists in the Old Trafford area. This building was next to the Botanical Gardens (White City) just off Chester Road, and the Police Headquarters are on that same spot now

HENSHAW'S BLIND ASYLUM AND DEAF AND DUMB SCHOOLS, OLD TRAFFORD, MANCHESTER.

WORKSHOPS FOR THE BLIND, DEANSGATE, MANCHESTER.

(From a Photograph by Our Own Artist.)

Henshaw's Blind Society decided to expand the workshops they ran in Salford and take advantage of the many empty spaces in the middle part of Deansgate. They built this handsome building for £11,000 and here 27 blind men and 5 blind women wove willow into baskets of all shapes and sizes, which went for sale in the shop fronting on to Deansgate. There were on piecework and could earn 16s 8d or more, although an average weekly wage was around 10/-

One of the finer buildings lost during Mr Hitler's reorganisation of the city. It is difficult to place where the Victoria Buildings were. To help the bottom left is the entrance to St. Ann's Square, the building on the middle right is where the Ramada Hotel is and you can just make out Exchange Station Building in the background, to the left. It was a very fine example of a Victorian shopping arcade, it contained 28 shops, 88 offices, 48 cellars plus a 231 room Hotel. There was a courtyard in the centre and over 1,500ft of balcony around it with a wonderful glass dome. When this picture was taken in February 1890 the building had just been finished, the shops were just being taken and the hotel was getting ready to open in the April.

VICTORIA BUILDINGS, MANCHESTER.

THE ATHENÆUM, MANCHESTER.

The Athenaeum Club was formed in October 1835 from an idea by John Walker a surgeon. It was formed to give the young men of Manchester a place to better themselves, to meet and discuss with their equals and to improve and entertain them. On October 23rd 1839 they had opened and paid for their own building in Princess Street. A fire early on the morning of September 24th 1873 destroyed most of the library and nearly all the rest of the building but it was eventually rebuilt. Princess Street was named when the Town Hall was built but it had had many other names including Brook Street (down to the river), Bond Street and the bit alongside the Art Gallery, David Street.

DEVIATION OF ROADWAY, OLD TRAFFORD.

It is very hard to imagine the impact that the Ship Canal had on Manchester. Every aspect of city life was transformed by its opening, and 100 years ago saw the height of anticipation. Salford was a mass of building and re-building. The Race Course was being moved to allow the new docks to be dug out. Road and railways were being diverted and every week brought something new connected with 'The Canal' (swing bridges, aquaducts etc.,).

A picture of Trafford Road, Salford being moved to align with the new swing bridge. When work started Abel Heywood and his new wife lived in a big house to the left of this picture in Throstles' Nest, three months later they had moved to Bowdon out of the "confounded noise and mud of the immense construction".

Wood and blood were said to be the main ingredients of the Ship Canal and this picture of Barton Locks taken in 1890 shows something of the scale of construction.

UNLOADING SLUICE PIERS, BARTON LOCKS.

DANIEL ADAMSON

March 1890 saw the passing of a man who had been at the very centre of the Ship Canal project and without whom it may not have been built. He lived in Didsbury at The Towers but was born in 1820 in Shildon in Durham and used to tell the story of how he remembered the opening day of the Stockton-Darlington Railway in 1825 and indeed was a pupil of Timothy Hackworth the railway engineer. Much was written on his demise about the frailty of life and how he had not seen his dream of ocean-going ships berthing at Throstles' Nest realised. Daniel Adamson Road behind the defunct Bus Depot on Eccles New Road seems a very poor memorial to a very far-seeing man. Though now a new office block by Throstle's Nest is named Adamson House — pity they lost the Daniel

LOCK-WORK AT MODE WHEEL.

Construction in Salford was the talking point and 100 years ago in the summer of 1893 most Sundays would see the road to that part blocked with sightseers and walkers going to see for themselves the wonder of the world being constructed right on their doorstep. Mind you there was plenty to look at as this photograph of Mode Wheel Locks shows.

MR. BOSDIN T. LEECH.
(Mayor-Elect of Manchester.)
(From a Photograph by Mr. M. Guttenberg.)

November 1st 1891 saw the distinguished figure of Mr Bosdin T. Leech to Mayor. When Daniel Adamsom died, even though Lord Egerton of Trafford took over the position of chairman it had been Bosden Leech who had taken up the fight to keep the project going. His diary of the every-day events with the building of the Canal published in two volumes have been a wonderful source of information to historians ever since.

He must have been a character of high standing as he was on the Stretford Committee to sell land needed to the Ship Canal Company and also on the Committee to buy the land for the building of the canal, yet no one seems to have cried out about the conflict of interests as they would today. He did much for Stretford, Flixton and Urmston and left behind a very good history book on the area.

BARTON AQUEDUCT, RIVER IRWELL.

A century ago saw the start of work to replace this fine stone bridge that carried Brindley's Canal over the River Irwell to the swinging aqueduct we have known for so long. At first it was proposed to build a lift, but the plans were changed and the Bridgewater Canal was diverted over the new 'marvel'. At the moment work has just started on a new crossing on very similar lines to the one rejected 100 years ago.

The Duke of Bridgewater built the Worsley Court House two hundred years ago, a hundred years before this photograph was taken. The black and white building was home of the Court for the area as well as a Lecture Theatre and Concert Hall. The Duke was a very benevolent man who left his mark very much on the village, from the clock which strikes 13 instead of one at lunch-time, to two churches he built at Worsley and Walkden. When he died in 1803 the village went to pieces and was for the next 20 years "a God-forsaken place with its inhabitants much taken with drink and rude sport to match their low morals".

COURT HOUSE, WORSLEY.
(From a Photograph by Mr. W. Blakeley.)

32

At the time of our photograph, Worsley was just a little orderly village north of Manchester. The name of Worsley came from Worked-lighs or Workesleys (worked or tilled fields not been turned before) and the village has many ancient connections, including a Roman Road running through it. Queen Victoria came to Worsley in 1851 and the Royal couple were conveyed from the Royal train at Patricroft Station by barge to Worsley where she disembarked at the Boat House, shown here, specially built for the occasion.

THE BOAT HOUSE, WORSLEY.
(From a Photograph by Mr. W. Blakeley.)

This is the area known then (and now) as St. Mary's Gate dominated by the clock tower on the second Exchange. Taken from Deansgate looking up Market Street, the creation of Corporation Street is still to come and the main road off was Exchange Street/Victoria Street on the left and St. Ann's Square on the right. That is the new Victoria Buildings just showing on the left.

The picture of Prestwich Parish Church which appeared in the March 1890 edition of Manchester Faces & Places, was there to celebrate the fact that the church had just finished a restoration and refurbishment.

Prestwich itself was still cut off and had a broad green belt between itself and Manchester. The name seems to come from Priests Retreat — Prestwych, and there were strong religious connections in the area. The Rev. W.T. Jones was the Rector when this photograph was taken, and the church was under the patronage of the Earl of Wilton from nearby Heaton Park. Thomas Henshaw benefactor of Henshaw's Blind Asylum and Oldham Blue Coat School is buried here.

PRESTWICH CHURCH, NEAR MANCHESTER.

HYDE ROAD PRISON.

From a refurbishment to a demolition, this fortress did not last 50 years: This is the large Hyde Road Prison which was closed and its inmates moved out after surveyors found the foundations unsafe and cracking due to subsidence. Built in 1847 as a short term and holding prison it opened for business two years later. In 1890 the building went up for auction, after the council had declined to buy it from the Government for £90,000. It was a strange auction, which attracted much attention, the building ended up being dismantled and carted away by various local builders. The prisoners' exercise tread mills (£110) and the punishment crank all sold, even the door of the cell which held the three Feinian prisoners connected with the Hyde Road Tragedy sold. In all only £5,000 was raised at the auction.

Telephones were spreading and the new-fangled means of communication was being accepted more and more. With the advent of telephones there were redundancies and sackings amongst the 'runners' who were employed to take messages from department to department in the larger firms and in the town hall. In 1895 telephones were still considered only for businesses, bosses and upper classes, people could not see them ever being available to the middle or working classes.

This "Centre for the exchange of electrical conversation" as it was referred to, was on the top floor of the Royal Exchange. The ladies at the far end wrote out the 'tickets' recording the calls. For local calls you were only charged for the call itself, not the length of time. Trunk calls (remember that expression — "I wish to make a trunk call") were important enough to have their own table. There were around 1,600 subscribers 100 years ago.

SWITCH ROOM, TELEPHONIC EXCHANGE.
(Central Office.)
(From a Photograph by Mr. W. E. Hutchinson, Chorlton-cum-Hardy.)

Two views of the fine black and white timbered building that was Agecroft Hall. Built in the time of Elizabeth the First, on the banks of the River Irwell (once a wonderful fishing river full of trout, chub, dace, gudgeons, and eels). The Langley family were the original owners of the Hall.

AGECROFT HALL. COURTYARD VIEW.

KERSAL CELL, NEAR MANCHESTER.
(From a Photograph by Mr. E. W. Wilkinson, Lower Broughton.)

Facing Agecroft across the River Irwell was the ancient building of Kersal Cell. The Cell, part of the name comes from a monastic settlement of the Cluniac Monks of Lenton who owned this land.

Kersal Cell will always be linked with the name of John Byrom the writer, famous for his hymn "Christians Awake!" and his connections with the Jacobite cause. Another famous family linked with the Jacobites, who lived in Kersal Cell before Byrom, were the Siddalls.

What a fine large expanse of water made up the ornamental lake complete with island in Alexandra Park. The building in the picture is St. Bede's College which believe it or not was originally built as an Aquarium for the study of unusual fish! The Park cost the corporation £60,000 to lay out and open for the benefit of the residents of Chorlton and Hulme. The Moss Side population who at this time were refusing to join the City of Manchester were enjoying these amenities free of charge. This caused much argument, and 100 years ago there were letters to the papers suggesting charging entrance fees to the Moss Siders and outsiders or forcing the Moss Side Corporation to pay towards its upkeep.

ALEXANDRA PARK.

(Entrance Gates, Alexandra Park.)

(From a Photograph by Mr. Albert Harris, Moss Side.)

Alexandra Park was so grand and so spacious, it was once described as the "Lungs of Manchester — bringing fresh air to the grime of an industrial City". In the spring 1893 a young lady writing in a local magazine tells how she had wandered into the park from the bustle and crowded shops of Alexandra Road and spent a pleasant hour strolling down the Grand Avenue pictured here. "Then listening to the birds and watching children and their nannies and nurses feeding the many ducks on the lake passed and improved the shining hours of the day".

The Gates of the park and the Head Park Keepers house. Can you make out the beautiful Clock Tower in the centre of the drive? There were plenty of drinking fountains dotted around the Park. There was once two gymnasiums, one boys, and one girls, and huge greenhouses in the Park.

ST. BEDE'S COLLEGE.
(From a Photograph by Messrs. Poulton & Sons, Lee, Kent.)

This building was opened as 'The Manchester Aquarium' in 1873. Great tanks were fitted with glass sides, and sea-water was brought in barrels from Blackpool on horse and carts, to supply the strange and exotic species exhibited. The public did not take to this new phenomena as they had in other cities, and the project folded within three years. The tanks were empty and the place deserted when Dr. Vaughan, Bishop of Salford, found the building and transformed it into a centre of learning. The statues were added to the brickwork and the building blessed and opened on 29th October 1878.

OUR BUSINESS PLACES. NO. 1.—MESSRS. OLLIVANT & BOTSFORD,
ST. ANN STREET.

A VANISHED CORNER.

From being granted a small town status under Salford to becoming a major city all in under 100 years shows the amount of wealth generated in the boom years of the cotton and manufacturing industries. St. Ann's Square and the surrounding streets became the fashionable shopping area for the rich, and many fine shops which were equal to any in London began to appear. Ollivant and Botsford, was already a well-established jewellers with premises in St. Mary's Gate (see above), but moved to St. Ann Street to larger premises in 1892 where it enjoyed a prime position, selling expensive jewellery and gifts.

The benefits of being able to relax and take recreation was very much in 'vogue' this time last century. It is hard to imagine just how popular the parks were. They were the only bit of greenery that some people ever saw, and councils prided themselves in the amenities that they provided for the local people. Bandstands, boating lakes, duck ponds, lovely gardens, fountains.

There were large Botanical Gardens at Old Trafford created after the Great Exhibition (which Prince Albert himself helped to organise). 'The Botanical & Horticultural Society' was formed to look after the needs of the Gardens. This picture from 1894 shows just how large the Palm House was. It was originally the Royal Dining room for the Exhibition and contained a Concert Hall within the acres of glass.

MR. BRUCE FINDLAY.
(Royal Botanical Gardens, Manchester.)
(From a Photograph by M. Guttenberg.)

PALM HOUSE AT THE ROYAL BOTANICAL GARDENS, MANCHESTER.

Superintendent of the Botanical Gardens was Mr Bruce Finlay. He lived in a modest lodge at the Stretford Road entrance and was the driving force behind its success, insisting on opening it more and more to the public. He spent 32 years in his beloved gardens

PALM HOUSE, BOTANICAL GARDENS, MANCHESTER.

An inside shot of the Palm House which attracted thousands of visitors in its time. The whole world was scoured to provide plants for the exotic displays.

LAKE SCENE AT ROYAL BOTANICAL GARDENS, MANCHESTER.

Lancashire Independent College was a beautiful creative building that could only enhance its purpose of training the cream of Lancashire's youth for the ministry. In 1840 the need for pastors was recognised and land in Whalley Range owned by Samuel Brooks was bought and the Teaching College built in only 3 years.

LANCASHIRE INDEPENDENT COLLEGE, MANCHESTER.

The top of King Street and the building that looks down over King Street was the Lancashire & Yorkshire Bank Building. When it was built in 1890 the main criticism of its fine facade was that the tall tower and an Italian Renaissance topping confused the outline and it would have been much better with just the Tower centred over the the street below. This lovely building with its wonderfully ornate interior, is now standing empty, waiting for some scheme to return it to its former glory.

LANCASHIRE AND YORKSHIRE BANK, SPRING GARDENS.
(From a Photograph by J. Duffie.)

47

If ever an old Hall was endowed with mixed fortunes, yet survives still, Ordsall Hall must hold the first prize. Whether historians like it or not, and whether Salford Council admit to it, the name of Harrison Ainsworth and his popular novel 'Guy Fawkes' definitely added interest to the place, and its mysteries are now forever intermingled. The Radcliffe family who lived here during the reign of Henry VIII and Queen Elizabeth I were a swashbuckling lot, who gave the Hall a lot of glory. The name appears for the first time as 'Hordeshal' in 1251, then in it was referred to as Ordesdale in 1296 and Ordsall in 1347. The council now own the Hall and it is open to the public.

The name New Cross seems to be forgotten now-a-days, but 100 years ago it was a well known and well defined area. It was the cross-roads at the top of Oldham Street with Swan Street and Ancoats. This picture shows Howard's extensive musical warehouse that sold all manner of instruments including zithers and mandolins. This looked down on the Cross that figured so much in the Peterloo trials. It was at New Cross that the reformers halted before marching on to Peterloo for the meeting, and it was the fact that they arrived marching in ranks and that a bugle halted and started them off again that figured against them at their trial.

BUSINESS PLACES. NO. 3.—A HISTORICAL CORNER.
(From a Photograph by J. Emsley, Pendleton).

ST. MARY'S CHURCH, MANCHESTER.
(From a Photograph by J. Ambler.)

There were many arguments going on about the demolition of the Church of St. Mary's that gave its name to St. Mary's Gate. Many opposed the demolition of this Church, which was hastened by its congregation moving over to the more fashionable St. Ann's in the Square. The Church was situated behind Kendals approximately where Henry's Wine Bar is today. Of course its name still lives on in St. Mary's Parsonage, and Parsonage Gardens today are the flags on the right of this picture. A 100 years ago the Church was still standing, but empty and awaiting its fate.

BARLOW HALL, NEAR MANCHESTER.

(From a Photograph by A. G. Heys, Hulme.)

Barlow Hall was one of the ancient family seats or halls that were dotted around Manchester in the 1890s. The Barlow family built the Hall in the 14th century and lived there until 1785, when it passed into other hands. Today the Hall, after centuries of mixed fortunes is the club house of Chorlton Golf Club.

Some Halls have one ghost, but this Hall is reputed to have three of them. There was also a gun kept on the wall that was not to be taken down: if ever it was removed the servants would not stay the night "as a bad tempered lady would appear with her head underneath her arm" to ensure a frightening night for all concerned.

Sir William Cunliffe Brooks lived in Barlow Hall a century ago. Well liked and well respected, an old and seasoned M.P., a Justice of the Peace for Manchester and Chester and Deputy Leuitenant of Lancashire. He was one of the Brooks family who moved down from Whalley in Lancashire and gave their name to Brooks Bar and to Whalley Range in South Manchester.

The 'great show piece' of Market Street was the description given to Lewis's Department Store. Lewis's was the first Department Store in the City, and people came from all over the county to window shop or make a purchase from this new, innovative "cash only" departmental store. Newspapers at the time were excited by the atmosphere that Lewis's Store generated and many said this was the way forward, and soon there would be many stores in Manchester. This was the first building to have electric lights which were run from a generator in the basement. Electricity from the mains was still a few years off (1903), and many buildings were having wires installed ready for the supply.

BUSINESS PLACES.--LEWIS'S, MARKET ST.
(From a Photograph by J. Emsley, Pendleton).

HEATON HALL, NEAR MANCHESTER.

(From a Photograph by Poulton & Son, Lee, Kent.)

The home or seat of the Earl of Wilton, Heaton Park in a fine view from 1893. Now a public park, this picture was taken when it was still a private home and the house was run by the Earl's sister Lady Alice de Voeux. Heaton Hall was always closely connected with Prestwich Church and they held the manor for some time.

This is the City Art Gallery started in 1825 and completed in 1830 at a total cost of £30,000. Designed by Sir Charles Barry (the architect of the Houses of Parliament) the building was of Ionic proportions, though it must be said that it has never been an imposing building. Still worth a visit today as it holds paintings by many of the city's famous artistic sons.

CITY ART GALLERY, MOSLEY STREET, MANCHESTER.

(From a Photograph by Poulton & Sons, Lee, Kent.)

Just one of the Jewish Synagogues on Cheetham Hill Road, this one was called the 'Great Synagogue'. At the end of the last century the Jewish community were well established in Manchester and had organised a Jewish Board of Guardians to support their own unfortunates. Guide books from this time last century always point out the multi-racial influences on the area. There were Synagogues for Spanish Jews (now the Jewish Museum), Portuguese Jews and this new one for British Jews complete with its 'Beth Hamidrash' (house of learning) which was in the basement

The Cheetham Hill Free Library was adjoining the Synagogue (to the left) and at this time was lending nearly 400 books a day.

The building with two domes on the far left is also a synagogue.

CHEETHAM HILL SYNAGOGUE & FREE LIBRARY.
(From a Photograph by J. Duffie, Ardwick.)

The trams were still horse-drawn and the Cathedral had not yet
got its extra porch on the front when this photograph was taken
from the Victoria Hotel looking towards Strangeways. The first
building on the right is still there, the second one built over the
old Hanging Ditch next to the Cathedral has gone. The Exchange
Station and its four storey building opened only 10 years before
on Monday 30th June 1884 was actually white when built, but
soon went grimy. The bombing of Manchester on 23rd December
1940 saw this building destroyed.

EXCHANGE STATION AND CROMWELL STATUE.

The Cromwell statue was the brainchild of Thomas Goadsby, but it was not until after his death that his wife (now Mrs Abel Heywood)
had Matthew Noble carry out his plan. This gave her immense pleasure as the statue overlooked the spot where Thomas had saved her from
the river at the launch of her father's ship 'The Emma' many years before. Cromwell was presented to the city on Wednesday 1st December
1875 and at the time it was said to be the best likeness known of the Parliamentarian. The pedestal alone weighed 16 tons and was brought
from a quarry at Penrhyn, Cornwall. Oliver can be found pedestal and all in Wythenshawe Park today.

AGECROFT AQUEDUCT, NEAR MANCHESTER.
(From a Photograph by J. W. Welch.)

The bridge that was built to carry the Manchester, Bolton & Bury Canal over the River Irwell. It was here that the river over-flowed its banks with alarming regularity. The narrow canal had been built a hundred years earlier in 1791 and was more than 15 miles long.

The Right Reverend Dr. Moorhouse was the Bishop of Manchester (the third one) at the time of this photograph. He was a Sheffield man who strangely came to Manchester via Melbourne Australia, having spent 10 years from 1876 to 1886 as Bishop of Melbourne, with a diocese which extended over many thousands of square miles. This hardworking, scholarly Yorkshireman was widely respected throughout Lancashire.

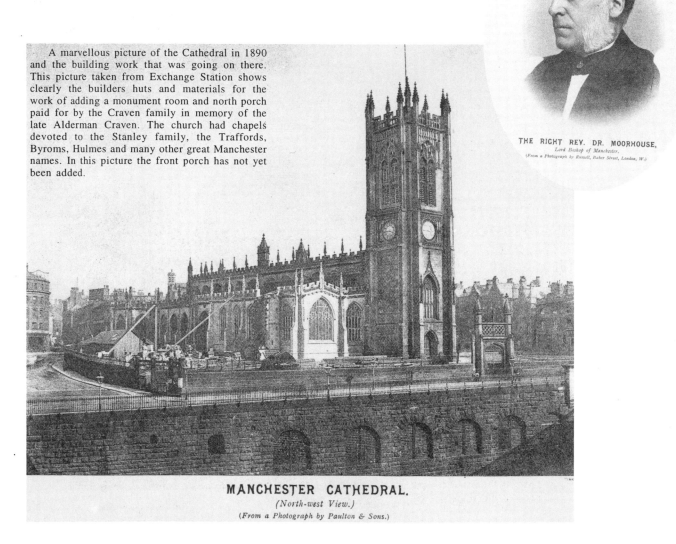

A marvellous picture of the Cathedral in 1890 and the building work that was going on there. This picture taken from Exchange Station shows clearly the builders huts and materials for the work of adding a monument room and north porch paid for by the Craven family in memory of the late Alderman Craven. The church had chapels devoted to the Stanley family, the Traffords, Byroms, Hulmes and many other great Manchester names. In this picture the front porch has not yet been added.

THE RIGHT REV. DR. MOORHOUSE,
Lord Bishop of Manchester.
(From a Photograph by Russell, Baker Street, London, W.)

MANCHESTER CATHEDRAL.
(North-west View.)
(From a Photograph by Paulton & Sons.)

More additions to the Cathedral in 1892 and here another porch is being added to the south side towards the City. Only 50 years before more than one writer remarked that "the newly elevated Manchester Cathedral looks more like a village parish church than the religious centre of a major city." This really struck home, and before long the wealthy families were using their wealth to add to and improve their new Cathedral with stained glass windows, statues, new porches, and many other memorials, to make their Cathedral one to be proud of. Note the wide Cathedral flags made up of headstones of the past.

The Grand Organ was part of the upgrading of the Cathedral. Designed by Sir Gilbert Scot and erected in 1872. Technically superb it ranked at 10th Church Organ in the country.

CATHEDRAL, MANCHESTER
(South View).

PRUDENTIAL ASSURANCE BUILDINGS, KING STREET, MANCHESTER.
(From a Photograph by W. H. Fischer, Withington.)

The top half of King Street was always the commercial part and completely unlike the lower end. The top half was also continually changing and a century ago a new building had appeared in the Prudential Assurance Building, designed by the celebrated artists who designed the Town Hall, Mr. Alfred Waterhouse.

Today as you go around the roundabout at the start of the M602 you cannot help but notice the Spire without a church. A landmark for many years to come, this is a great opportunity to place on record the reason for building the original church. The Stowell Memorial Church (pictured here) was built in commemoration of the life and labours of the Rev. Canon Hugh Stowell. Born in Douglas, Isle of Man in 1799 he did great work with the poor people of Salford whilst at St. Stephens Church, Salford. Nothing could induce him to leave Salford, even in ill health he carried on, until his death in 1865; The whole of Salford turned out to say farewell to him, the bishop and over 200 clergy headed the mile long procession of mourning for this oft unsung hero.

STOWELL MEMORIAL CHURCH, SALFORD.
(From a Photo by Mr. J. Ambler, Manchester.)

THE REV. CANON T. A. STOWELL, M.A.
(From a Photograph by Brown, Barnes & Bell, Manchester and Liverpool.)

Canon Thomas Stowell was the son of Hugh Stowell. Born in Bolton Street, Salford, he followed in his fathers footsteps, and after various parishes accepted the appointment as rector of Christ Church Salford. He continued the families good work and helped build up Salford's schools and Sunday schools, which were attended by over 2,000 children every Sunday. He continued for 24 years until, stepping aside for a younger man, he went off to be Dean of Leyland.

Rev. William Muzzell, the Rector of St. Mark's Church in Holland Street, Ancoats, was incensed at the conditions under which the people in his parish lived.

He wrote in 1892 "our atmosphere is dense with smoke and laden with poison from innumerable chimneys, chemical works, and so many other works of an offensive nature . . . the City Health Works (refuge department) deals with 625 carts of rubbish per day, the Bradford Gas Works, the Alum Works, the Glue Factory, the Soap and Bone Works, the Horse Slaughtering Works etc., all add to the bad stench over Ancoats where the death rate is higher than anywhere else in the kingdom . . ."

He instigated help for the people of the area and this coincided with a flush of charitable works in Manchester, and resulted in the People's Institute, shown here, opening in 1889. It was the first of its kind built to "infuse light into a poor area". The basement had a large soup kitchen and enamel baths for men and women (in an area where no dwelling had a fitted bath). For a penny a hot bath and towel could be had, with reductions for whole families going together!

This was immensely popular especially on the Saturday before Whit Monday in 1891, when 305 people had a bath that day, and a total of 8,000 baths were taken that year. The ground floor had a Reading Room, Small Library, a Job Club and Writing Room, with instruction to teach reading and writing to adults who wished. Instruction was also given in sewing, knitting and other skills.

THE PEOPLE'S INSTITUTE, HOLLAND STREET, ANCOATS, MANCHESTER.
(From a Photograph by Mr. J. Ambler.)

LABORERS' DWELLINGS SCHEME,
OLDHAM ROAD, MANCHESTER.
(From a Photograph.)

Part of the improvements in the Ancoats area in the 1890s was the building of the Victoria Dwellings, which still survive today. This picture from 1891 shows the shops on the right of Oldham Road that are about to be cleared by order of the 'Unhealthy Dwelling Committee' set up by Manchester Corporation to provide a 'healthier city'.

This was how the church of the Holy Name and Oxford Road looked 100 years ago. The original building was so small and plain it was nicked-named 'The Shed', but then due to the extraordinary efforts of a Father Vaughan money was raised not only for a larger church, but also a Meeting House. A remarkable gathering entitled 'Rome in Manchester' was held on October 14th 1890 in the fields behind Oxford Road, opened by the Marquis of Ripon, it raised £6,500 towards the fund including a substantial amount paid by Sir Humphrey de Trafford for a full sized likeness of Pope Leo XIII presented by the Pope himself which was later hung in the Hall.

The Reverend Bernard Vaughan who worked so hard and tirelessly for the good of his community. Very astute, very eloquent, and described as good looking, Father Vaughan came from a very old, strong Catholic family. Educated at Stoneyhurst College he had a great gift for enthusing his audience, and his sermons were always well attended, up to 3,000 people packed in at times to listen to him.

Not to be confused with his brother Herbert who was the Right Reverend Bishop of Salford.

REV. BERNARD VAUGHAN, S.J.
(Church of the Holy Name, Manchester)

CHURCH OF THE HOLY NAME, OXFORD STREET, MANCHESTER.
(From a Photograph by Messrs. Poulton & Sons, Lee, Kent.)

BROUGHTON PARK CHURCH.
(From a Photograph by Mr. E. W. Wilkinson, Lower Broughton.)

When the Committee of the Lancashire & Cheshire Congregationalist Chapels decided to support the plan to erect a Congregational Church in the area of Higher Broughton there was unexpected opposition. The Trustees of the Clowes Estate objected to any non-conformist place of worship in Broughton Park, and it was only after some time they allowed the purchase of a plot of land in 1872. By 1893, the time of this picture, the church had grown and had a branch church in Rooden Lane with its own school, and also a church school at the Cheetham Hill entrance of Broughton Park. This church was considered the finest non-conformist place of worship in the whole country, a hundred years ago. Today it stands empty and derelict.

Sometimes as a city or an area develops, bits of that city seem to get left out, overlooked, and charming timeless pockets are suddenly thrust into the limelight. This is what happened with the Cheetwood area and Cheetwood Village a hundred years ago. Suddenly it was in all the papers and journals that here was a little bit of old Manchester that the developers had passed by. It became a place to walk out to, to see. Cheetwood was the area above Strangeways Prison, the area above Derby Street going up to Elizabeth Street. All that is left of the area now is the name Cheetwood Street, and Cheetham Park with a rare Bandstand. The Strangeways Tower helps place the picture.

CHEETWOOD VILLAGE.
(From a Photograph by Mr. T. H. Newsome, Rydal Mount, Cheetham.)

ECCLES CHURCH.

(From a Photograph by Mr. Wm. Blakeley, Pendleton.)

Eccles is one of the oldest parts of the area and the name is world renowned through the 'Eccles Cake'. The Parish Church dedicated to St. Mary was built on the site of churches going back to the 12th century and had been added to and repaired many times in the 1800's ending in a wholly renovated and restored Parish Church in 1862.

An 1892 picture of the building on the corner of Brown Street and King Street which was the Manchester Reform Club. Opened at a cost of £60,000, it housed every convenience for 'gentlemen' plus one of the finest billiard rooms in Manchester.

REFORM CLUB, KING STREET.
(From a Photograph by Messrs. Poulton & Sons, Lee, Kent.)

Clayton Hall was bought by Humphrey Chetham in 1620 for £4,700 along with land in Failsworth, Ashton, Woodhouses and Droylsden. He lived here right up until his death in 1653 and ran his empire and duties from the Hall. At the time of this picture the Hall still had its moat around it, but the drawbridge has been replaced by a stone bridge.

CLAYTON HALL, NEAR MANCHESTER.
(From a Photograph by Miss Rosa Scott.)

POET'S CORNER, LONG MILLGATE.
(From a Photograph by Mr. Henry Sykes.)

Although cleared now there was in 1893 one area of Manchester which had remained untouched for many years. This area was on Long Millgate, just opposite the entrance to Chethams College. The row of houses pictured here contained the Sun Inn (Poets Corner), the oldest house in Manchester and the school tuck shop. Long Millgate was the main road into central Manchester before Corporation Street was laid out. The name 'Poets Corner' came about because one of the landlords of the Sun Inn a William Earnshaw, himself a scholar, invited the interested gentlemen of Manchester to a poetical soiree in January 1842 and the Inn became the meeting place of the men dubbed as the Manchester Poets. Charles Swain (the sweetest voice in Lancashire) John C. Prince, J.B. Rogerson, Sam Bamford and many more were long connected with the Sun Inn which had the words Poets Corner then engraved over the entrance.

HOUSES IN LONG MILLGATE.
(From a Photograph by Mr. Henry Sykes.)

There is only one building left on Long Millgate today — The Post Office and Flower Stall, but 100 years ago there were houses from Fennel Street right up to Ducie Bridge and beyond. Many famous names have been connected with this thoroughfare. One that cannot be passed over as he lived in one of these houses pictured here is Joshua Brooks the famous clergyman who was said to have married and baptized more people than any other clergyman. He used to organise mass weddings on bank holidays and 20-40 couples would gather before him in the Parish Church (the Cathedral) to be married in one service. One story which I am sure is true, is that one Whit Monday he told the couples waiting to be married to pair off and line up only to find that there were 42 women and only 41 men. He told the lonely bride that she was going through with the marriage anyway and insisted that the man he married first, go and take the place of the missing groom and be married again. After the service the new bride was sent off to the Sun Inn where the reluctant groom was located to tell him that he was well and truly spliced in his absence! The Rev. Joshua Brooks was also not averse to changing the names of children as he baptised them. With his many eccentricities he became one of Manchester's Great Characters*.

* See The Manchester Man.

SALFORD ROYAL HOSPITAL.
(From a Photograph by Mr. George Wheeler.)

One hundred years ago Salford was very proud of its hospital and the sterling work it was doing in raising the standard of care in the district. It received its Royal title from the attention of Prince Albert, and indeed the corner stone was laid on April 23rd (his birthday) in 1830. When the hospital was completed Prince Albert contributed £250 per annum to its upkeep, although most of the money came from local beneficiaries. This is now a very sad building, empty and boarded up, with Salford missing the attention it so long and so well provided.

Manchester's main Post Office was in Brown Street near to the banking and commercial centre of King Street, which provided so much of their work. The building cost an enormous £120,000. and was one of the most imposing buildings in Manchester. Built of Portland Stone to a design by a government surveyor, a Mr Williams, its 246ft long facade was built by Robert Neill & Sons. In 1893, 1,600 people worked for the Post Office, and it had takings of over £10,000 per week in stamps, 2,000,000 million letters and parcels were handled there every week while 150,000 telegrams (including press messages) passed through this building.

MANCHESTER POST OFFICE, BROWN STREET.
(From a Photograph by Mr. J. Duffie.)

A very handsome building which had just been completed and opened on 1st May 1891. The National Provincial Bank in Spring Gardens at the top of King Street was the very latest and ornate of buildings. Another design by Alfred Waterhouse, and built on the site of the former Manchester Telegraphic Offices. The Bank itself was only in the Main Hall at street level, the three stories, above being offices for the Ship Canal Company, who were busy sorting out details of their Salford and Manchester building operations.

NATIONAL PROVINCIAL BANK, SPRING GARDENS.
(From a Photograph by Our Own Artist.)

This was the original Kendal Milne Building as it was in 1894. This building is now Waterstone's bookshop. The fashionable ladies would alight from their carriages in Police Street, at the back of the store, to enter the 'elegantly-appointed emporium with its choicest novelties and 'lifts' that deliver you you to the floor you want'. Kendals also had the premises where they are today, and the furniture shown there included the Royal Receiving Rooms from the Jubilee Exhibition. Three gentlemen (Thomas Kendal, James Milne and Adam Faulkner) bought the business from J.S. & J. Watts, and set up as Kendal, Milne & Faulkner on 26th December 1835. Mr Faulkner died in 1862, and in 1865 the firm was renamed Kendal, Milne & Co.

THE LATE MR. THOMAS KENDAL.
(From a Photograph by M. Saury.)

Mr Thomas Kendal died in July 1891, and his sons Herbert and Sam who were firmly established in the business took over the reins smoothly. Mr Kendal came from Kendal in the Lake District, he previously lived and worked in London and only came to Manchester when business in London became too hectic for him. He was a very staunch Congregationalist, and was intrumental in setting up Cheadle Church. He was buried at Heaton Mersey Congregational Burial Ground.

This time last century there was quite an argument over who made the first commercial Eccles Cakes and where they were made. With the benefits of time and research it is now easy to set the record straight. The picture shows the original premises, but with the pretenders in residence.

Birch's were the original makers and their shop was the one above, but it was too small and James Birch took premises across the road. Mr. Bradburn, a former worker at the shop, decided to take the old shop and opened it making 'Eccles Cakes'. He put up a sign saying "The Original Eccles Cake Shop". Birch was livid and within days had his own sign "Birch's the old-established Original Eccles Cake Shop, removed from the other side". This battle of the signs continued for many years and caused much merriment and wonder, with visitors stood in the middle of the road reading both signs and wondering which shop to go into. February 1891 saw the argument in the open again as Birch's shop was auctioned and it was said they made 30,000 Eccles Cakes a week.

THE "ORIGINAL ECCLES CAKE SHOP."
(From a Photograph by Mr. Wm. Blakeley, Pendleton.)

76

OLD HOUSE, MARKET PLACE, MANCHESTER.

(From a Photograph by Our Own Artist.)

Market Place in 1891. This corner building now the Wellington Inn at the back of Marks & Spencers has been many things in its time from a Fishing Tackle shop to an Opticians. One of its most famous inhabitants was John Byrom, author of 'Christians Awake' and erstwhile Jacobite*, who was born in this building.

* See Manchester Rebels £2.50 all good bookshops.

EXCHANGE STATION.
(From Cathedral Front.)
(From a Photograph by Our Own Artist.)

Exchange Station was opened in June 1884 to give London North Western its own station and take the pressure off Victoria Station next to it. It boasted the 'longest platform in the world' and at the time of our picture in 1892 direct trains from this station went to Carlisle, Scotland, Morecambe, Liverpool, North Wales, Newcastle, Hull and the Lakes as well as connecting services to London.

This is a very interesting picture taken in July 1892 showing Mount Street Manchester looking towards Albert Square. The buildings on the right were demolished for the Town Hall Extension and Library. The railings on the left belong to the Friends Meeting House built in 1828 which is still there and well used. The building on the left was used by the Inland Revenue Office at the time.

MOUNT STREET, MANCHESTER.
(From a Photograph by Messrs. Frith & Sons, Reigate.)

The Manchester Palace of Varieties was the full title of this grand ornate building. Designed by Alfred Darbyshire and F. Bennett Smith, it was built under Mr. Darbyshire's supervision, but amidst much opposition. The Railway Arms (by the railway bridge) complained that gunpowder blasting for the foundations made the glasses tremble and customers leave quickly and blasting was banned in opening hours. Darbyshire hit back by threatening to sack on the spot any workman found in the Railway Inn.

They wanted the very best at The Palace and imported Signor Morolda to oversee the Italian work on the ornate facade. He even built a special old marble door-way on the entrance to the balcony secured from a dismantled palazzo in Italy, and the staircases are Sicilian marble.

There was a great deal of opposition to the building of the Palace Theatre, it was thought that it would become a den of vice, especially if alcohol was allowed to be served. After many set backs, including a refusal to issue a Performing Licence, it finally opened, minus a liquor licence on May 16th 1891 to 3,000 people.

PALACE THEATRE OF VARIETIES, OXFORD ROAD, MANCHESTER.
(From a Photograph by Our Own Artist.)

Mr George Scott, Manager of the Palace Theatre when it opened 1891 had formerly been Manager of the Comedy Theatre. It was Mr Scott who booked the acts for the theatre and it was Mr Scott and his preference for Comedy and Pantomimes which brought success to this new venture.

MR. T. RAMSAY.
(Manager of the Theatre Royal.)
(From a Photograph by Mr. Warwick Brookes.)

This 1893 picture of the Theatre Royal in Peter Street, shows a strong square building that was at the heart of Manchester's entertainment scene. A newspaper article in 1890 stated "within half a mile of this building are theatres and places of entertainment to suit every taste, and a Saturday night can see as many as 30,000 people enjoying 'live' theatre". The Cinema was still 15 years away. Built at a cost of £23,000 in 1845 it replaced other Theatre Royals in Manchester, and opened on September 29th with a performance of the new comedy 'Time Works Wonders'. The theatre was closed in June 1889 and bought by Mr T. Ramsay, refurbished and refitted, it opened for the Pantomime season later that year. 1893 saw the D'Oyly Carte's Company, Henry Irving, the Gaiety Burlesque Company, Mrs Langtree and one Beerbohm Tree entertaining record crowds.

CONSERVATIVE CLUB, MANCHESTER.

(From a Photograph.)

This building is on the corner of St. Ann's Street and Cross Street was opened on 26th October 1876 at a cost of nearly £60,000 to build. There are many fine stained glass windows and murals in its wonderfully ornate interior.

DEANSGATE, MANCHESTER.
(From a Photograph by Messrs. Frith & Sons, Reigate.)

An 1894 picture of the head of Deansgate showing many horse-drawn omnibuses. The large building in the middle, is the Victoria Buildings and Hotel, which are now long gone. The Cathedral in the background helps place the picture. Deansgate is the most ancient of the main roads of Manchester. It is said to have been the highway of the Romans and part of Watling Street, the name Deansgate comes from the Rural Dean and the gateway into St. Michael's Church which was in this area before the Cathedral.

Cross Street Chapel as it appeared at the end of the last century. It is such a shame that this was one of the buildings destroyed during the War as its successor, though fine, is nothing like the original. This Chapel was built for Henry Newcome, the founder of Non-conformity in Manchester in 1694, and he preached his first sermon there that year. Cross Street Chapel was steeped in history and associations with many famous names in Manchester's history. A past Minister was the Rev. Ralph Harrison, whose only daughter Anne, married Thomas Ainsworth and William Harrison Ainsworth the popular novelist was one of their sons. It was William's attendance at this Chapel that brought his friend, Charles Dickens to worship here each Sunday, and Charles Dickens later told of the small cripple boy there who gave him the idea of 'Tiny Tim' for the novel he was writing called 'A Christmas Carol'. Another Minister with literary connection was William Gaskell, whose wife, Elizabeth Gleghorn Gaskell, enriched English literature with her novels — 'Cranford', 'Mary Barton' etc.

CROSS STREET CHAPEL, MANCHESTER.
(From a Photograph by Mr. Lafosse.)

OUR BUSINESS PLACES:
MR. JOHN HARROP, PICCADILLY, MANCHESTER.
(From a Photograph by Mr. John Ambler, Market Street, Manchester.)

John Harrop had started the business as a book publishing house only 25 years before this photo was taken in 1897. He added various departments to his retail book shop till this time last century his shops had separate departments for furniture, ironmongery, bath chairs and invalid furniture, bedsteads, bedding, drapery and soft goods, clocks and watches, cycles, travelling bags and trunks, jewellery, fancy goods, books and many others.

Our picture shows his store in Piccadilly with Bassinettes and mail carts as part of their 'Great Sale'

The company's main warehouse and head office was in Tib Street, Manchester and they had opened stores in Pendleton, Ashton-under-Lyne, Stockport, Oldham, Rochdale, Preston, Hyde and Warrington as well as a large factory in Bury Street Mills in Stockport, where hundreds of workers turned out household furniture as well as 7,000 infant carriages and carts per year.

YOUNG MEN'S CHRISTIAN ASSOCIATION, MANCHESTER.

The Young Men's Christian Association was flourishing in 1891 and had recently opened this hall in Peter Street where they remained for a hundred years. They had 2,400 members who enjoyed a Chess Club, a Rambling Club, and other clubs for swimming, athletics, art, photography and literature, as well as Evening Educational Classes. They handed out some relief to commercial men on hard times and also assisted over 1,500 young men to emigrate to Canada.

The YMCA was not always so successful, the first attempt in 1847 ended in them giving up their premises in George Street, but the committee never gave up and came back in the 1870's.

ALL SAINTS' CHURCH, MANCHESTER.

(From a Photograph by Messrs. Frith & Sons, Reigate.)

The name All Saints lives on as an area of Manchester, down Oxford Road, but at the end of the 1800's the church of All Saints' could be held up as a shining example of a church bringing together the upper classes of its community and doing so much for the ordinary parishioners. The rector started the All Saints' National Day School in York Street in 1820 and by 1895 it had four large classes in prosperous condition. There was also the Mission Church of St. Matthias in Sackville Street. The Church itself (shown in our picture) was built in 1820 when all around were green fields. After a fire in 1850 it was quickly repaired at a cost of £3,000. and re-opened within six months. The Sunday School was so popular with reading and writing lessons thrown in, that they had to hold two large sessions every Sunday. The All Saints' Benefit Society were doing much needed good "visiting, clothing and relieving the sick and the poor".

ST. PETER'S CHURCH, MANCHESTER.
(From a Photograph by Our Own Artist.)

There is not one of these buildings standing today, but our photograph shows St. Peter's Square a hundred years ago. The church had been consecrated in 1794 and was there until 1904 when it was finally demolished. The Cenotaph is now where the church spire stood, and tram tracks have returned to the square.

MANCHESTER CITY AMBULANCE.
(From a Photograph by Mr. Walter Mellor, Bury.)

ROYAL EYE HOSPITAL, MANCHESTER.
(From a Photograph by Messrs. Frith & Sons, Reigate.)

The Royal Eye Hospital on Oxford Road as it was in 1893. Opened only seven years before, it was much needed to replace the overflowing Eye Hospital in St. John's Street, Deansgate, that had been trying to cope with 12,961 out-patients, and 1,264 received into hospital in 1885.

Two terracotta panels facing Oxford Street, are worth mentioning 'Christ Healing the Blind' and 'Elymas Struck Blind' are the subjects. An Eye Hospital was started at the top of King Street in 1814 as "a public charity for the relief of the poor inflicted with diseases of the eye" and after various homes ended here in on the corner of Nelson Street.

GOLDSTONE DIAMOND MERCHANT *Watch Manufacturer & Jeweller*

£150 LIFE £150 17/6 MARVEL 17/6
INSURANCE POLICY SOLID SILVER WATCH
FOR TWELVE MONTHS AGAINST ALL RAILWAY ACCIDENTS WITH A WRITTEN WARRANTY FOR TWO YEARS
AND A LIFE INSURANCE POLICY FOR
£1 PER WEEK £1 FIFTY £50 POUNDS
FOR SIX WEEKS DURING DISABLEMENT AGAINST RAILWAY ACCIDENTS AND
GIVEN WITH EVERY ONE OF £1 PER WEEK £1
GOLDSTONES FAMOUS ENGLISH FOR SIX WEEKS IN CASE OF DISABLEMENT
LEVER WATCHES. IS PRESENTED ABSOLUTELY FREE WITH THE
FULL PARTICULARS ON APPLICATION. "MARVEL WATCH."

GOLDSTONES FAMOUS WATCHES

OUR BUSINESS PLACES.—NO. 11. GOLDSTONE'S, ST. MARY'S GATE.
(From a Photograph by Our Own Artist.)

Goldstone is a well known name in Manchester and this was the retail shop of S. Goldstone, Watch Manufacturer which stood on the corner of St. Mary's Gate. The firm also had wholesale premises in Exchange Buildings. The business started as wholesale only, nearly 60 years before, and watches were made on the premises. At the time of this picture if you purchased a watch from Goldstones' and were wearing it in a railway accident the Travellers Accident Insurance Company would pay between £50 and £150 in case of death, and £1. per week if disabled from business. There are no records of them ever paying a claim.

The Congregational Church on Chorlton Road at Brooks Bar was opened in 1861 and a very handsome building it was for the £8,000 it cost to build. Its complex included a fine school, a lecture room and other buildings. The church had the well-known and popular Dr Macfadyen as its Minister up until his death in 1899 and it was one of the largest and most influential in south Manchester. It was pulled down only a few years ago but there is still a small Worship Centre on the spot.

I had to include this picture as this is the church where I was married 21 years ago.

CHORLTON ROAD CONGREGATIONAL CHURCH.
(From a Photo by Mr. E. Ward, Manchester.)

1889 saw the opening of the Great Northern Railway's new Goods Depot at the bottom of Deansgate. To build this huge warehouse together with the shops underneath that front Deansgate, over one hundred slum dwellings were cleared, and the occupants compelled to find other places to live. Over £1,000,000 were spent in clearing and constructing this warehouse, but it brought the Great Northern Company right into the heart of the City. It was at the time one of the most important pieces of work carried out by any Railway Company.

GREAT NORTHERN RAILWAY COMPANY'S GOODS WAREHOUSE, MANCHESTER.

THE STORIES AND TALES SERIES

Stories and Tales Of Old Merseyside
(Frank Hird, edited Cliff Hayes)
Over 50 stories of Liverpool's characters and incidents PLUS a booklet from 1890 telling of the city's history, well illustrated.
ISBN 1 872226 20 5 £4.95

Stories & Tales Of Old Lancashire
(Frank Hird)
Over 70 fascinating tales told in a wonderful light-hearted fashion. Witches, seiges and superstitions, battles and characters all here.
ISBN 1 872226 21 3 £4.95

Stories and Tales Of Old Manchester
(Frank Hird, edited Cliff Hayes)
A ramble through Manchester's history, many lesser known stories brought to life, informative yet human book. Over 50 stories.
ISBN 1 872226 22 1 £4.95

NORTHERN CLASSIC REPRINTS

The Manchester Man
(Mrs. G. Linnaeus Banks)
Re-printed from an 1896 illustrated edition — undoubtedly the finest paperback edition ever. Fascinating reading, includes Peterloo. Over 400 pages, wonderfully illustrated.
ISBN 1 872226 16 7 £4.95

The Lancashire Witches
(W. Harrison Ainsworth)
A beautiful illustrated edition of the most famous romance of the supernatural.
ISBN 1 872226 55 8 £4.95

NOW £2.50 — BARGAIN!!!

The Manchester Rebels
(W. Harrison Ainsworth)
A heady mixture of fact and fiction combined in a compelling story of the Jacobean fight for the throne of England. Manchester's involvement and the formation of the Manchester Regiment. Authentic illustrations.
ISBN 1 872226 29 9 £4.95

Hobson's Choice (the Novel)
(Harold Brighouse)
The humorous and classic moving story of Salford's favourite tale. Well worth re-discovering this enjoyable story. Illustrated edition. Not been available since 1917, never before in paperback.
ISBN 1 872226 36 1 £4.95

The Dock Road
(J. Francis Hall RN)
A seafaring tale of old Liverpool. Set in the 1860s with the American Civil War raging and the cotton famine gripping Lancashire. Period illustrations.
ISBN 1 872226 37 X £4.95

NORTHERN CLASSIC REPRINTS

― POETRY COLLECTION ―

NOW £2.50

Poems & Songs of Lancashire

(Edwin Waugh)

wonderful quality reprint of a classic book by undoubtedly one of ncashire's finest poets. First published 1859 faithfully reproduced. Easy pleasant reading, a piece of history.

N 1 872226 27 2 £4.95

The Best of Old Lancashire
― Poetry & Verse

lished in 1866 as the very best of contemporary Lancashire writing, this k now offers a wonderful insight into the cream of Lancashire literature the middle of the last century. Nearly 150 years later, edited and blished, the book now presents a unique opportunity to read again the sters of our past.

N 1 872226 50 7 £4.95

Songs of a Lancashire Warbler

(Lowell Dobbs)

riendly and humorous book of new Lancashire poetry, very much in ping with the best of the past masters of the dialect and helping to keep e the heritage of the Lankysheer twang. A book written with insight and npassion, by Lowell Dobbs, winner of many awards for his art and a rising ster of dialect prose.

N 1 872226 49 3 £4.95

The History of Lancashire Cookery

Tom Bridge takes us deep into Lancashire's culinary past to reveal the classic dishes of the region.

ISBN 1 872226 25 6 £4.95

Includes a facsimile reprint of the U.C.P. Tripe Recipe Book from 1934.

Completely Lanky

(Dave Dutton)

Combining two best sellers - Lanky Panky and Lanky Spoken Here with additional copy.

ISBN 1 872226 61 2 £4 95

Cammell Laird ― The Golden Years

(Dave Roberts)

Well illustrated. A fully history of this great shipyard.

ISBN 1 872226 48 5 £4.95

For The Children

Poems & Stories by well-known authors and personalities. Produced for the Tay Sachs Society.

ISBN 1 872226 14 0 £4.95

Getting to Know…

Getting to Know…
THE LAKE DISTRICT

RON & MARLENE FREETHY

Getting to Know…
HIDDEN LANCASHIRE

RON & MARLENE FREETHY

also THE RIBBLE VALLEY, PENDLE, PEAK DISTRICT & SECRET LANCASHIRE

also *Greetings from…*

ECCLES, AROUND MANCHESTER, OLD SALFORD, YORKSHIRE COAST, LIVERPOOL, THE WIRRAL

Greetings from **THE NORTH WALES COAST**

Cliff Hayes

Greetings from **THE LANCASHIRE COAST**

Greetings from **THE HEART OF LANCASHIRE**

Catherine Rothwell and Cliff Hayes